SHIFTING PERSPECTIVES

ANTHONY SCHMIDT

Address all inquiries to: ramonaschmidt@outlook.com

Photography by Anthony Schmidt
Written by Anthony Schmidt and Ramona Schmidt
Photo editing by Scott Christenson
Graphic design by Graeme Hunt Design | graemehuntdesign.com

SHIFTING PERSPECTIVES
By Anthony Schmidt
ISBN: 978-1-63618-247-6
Library of Congress Control Number (LCCN): 2022920954

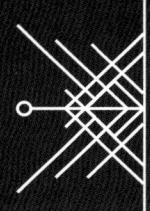

AVIVA
PUBLISHING
New York

Aviva Publishing
Lake Placid, NY
518-523-1320
avivapubs.com

Printed in the United States of America

First Edition
2 4 6 8 10 12

SHIFTING PERSPECTIVES

ANTHONY SCHMIDT

Left: 1957 Ford Fairlane
Right: 1959 Chevrolet Impala
St. Edward State Park
Kenmore, Washington

TABLE OF CONTENTS

SHIFTING PERSPECTIVES

If there's something Anthony teaches us, it's that life is all about perspectives. It's all a matter of how you look at things: big challenges can appear small when you look at them through a different lens.

Many times, on Anthony's autism journey, I, his mom, have noticed how taking time to see the world from his perspective has offered me moments of such beauty. That is what is so profound about Anthony's photography: the opportunity to see the world through his eyes. People often ask, "Why mention autism in connection with Anthony's photography?" They say, "He's a talented photographer; it should be irrelevant." To that I say, not mentioning Anthony's autism would be extremely dismissive of what he's gone through to get where he is today and what he still goes through daily. It also is dismissive of the hidden talents that sometimes come with autism.

I was there when his obsession with cars began. Without a doubt, I can say he wouldn't be doing this if it hadn't been for autism. It's because of autism, not despite it. If we didn't mention autism, it would be in a way admitting that having a diagnosis is something to be ashamed of. Anthony is changing the way people view autism. He is helping to remove the stigma of autism, and in that way, he's shifting perspectives in more ways than one.

1931 Ford Model A

Left: 1957 Cadillac Eldorado
Center left: 1954 Cadillac Eldorado
Center right: 1948 Chevrolet Fleetline
Right: 1958 Chevrolet Apache
Above: 1957 Mercedes 280SE
King Charley's Drive-In
Snohomish, Washington

King Charley's

Anthony woke up early one Sunday morning because he heard of a garage sale in Lake Stevens that was selling an entire collection of diecast cars. He cleared them out. On the way home, we stopped at this diner that looked perfect for the era of cars. Thankfully, they were closed that day so there were no out-of-era cars parked out front to ruin the illusion.

Left: 1948 Chevrolet Fleetline
Center: 1954 Cadillac Eldorado
Right: 1942 Ford F1
King Charley's Drive-In, Snohomish, WA

Left: 1948 Chevrolet Fleetline

Anthony had just purchased the latest version of the iPhone for himself and this was his first photoshoot with the new updated camera phone. The wide angle feature in the iPhone 13 Pro Max added one more element of realism to his photos and this set went viral on social media. Turns out the owner of King Charley's is a car enthusiast too, and he was thrilled to have Anthony shoot there.

Left: 1939 Chevrolet
Right: 1941 Chevrolet 3100
King Charley's Drive-In
Snohomish, Washington

Left: 1954 Cadillac Eldorado
Right: 1949 Buick Roadmaster
King Charley's Drive-In
Snohomish, Washington

1953 Chevrolet 3100

The River Road

Anthony had the idea to create a platform with a river. Initially, the idea was to pour real water in it, so we lined it with Flex Seal so it would hold water. As luck would have it, the Flex Seal ended up looking more like real water than the actual water did. So with that happy accident, we were able to make a very versatile river diorama that Anthony gets a lot of use out of. Especially stunning are the shots where the sun reflects off the river.

1959 Buick Electra

The Church in the Meadow

Anthony commissioned this church from talented artist Phillip Crews of Mount Pleasant, Tennessee. He made this just with Anthony in mind and put more than his usual detail into this building. The photos Anthony created with it have become fan favorites.

Above left: 1949 Buick
Above right: 1948 Chevrolet Fleetline

"How does a person describe the pictures that Anthony takes without sounding cliché, or worse condescending? I, personally, don't think there's enough words in any dictionary anywhere. The growth we have seen in his craft goes beyond mere words. His abilities to transform a model car into a full scale photo is nothing short of sheer genius. I have stared at his pictures for hours looking for the mistake, an error not in scale. And to no avail. Hence, I now admire, respect, and am left in total awe. A Dreamweaver. Our guide back to a simpler time. And all of us, if just for a minute or two, are caught off guard and let yesterday's memories flood in and bring us to smile and stroll down memory lane. I said once and I'll say it again... Anthony, you are the keeper of the keys and, yes, our Dreamweaver."

— *William Houser*

1925 and 1931
Ford Model T pickups

1948 Chevrolet

"Anthony's photographs tell a story. They draw you into a world that you wonder about, that Anthony has made up. So many artists try to accomplish that and fall short of what Anthony has already done! As to folks who don't understand that he puts in many hours of actual work into each series of photos, plus his time in creating the ideas, collecting the right cars and props, matching them with the appropriate historical setting—well, they may never understand! That is one thing all professional artists and professional photographers like Anthony Schmidt have in common, even the ones who have art degrees. Sort of like other professionals like lawyers who are paid for their time, ability, and know-how. There is always someone who doesn't understand the value of an artist's skill and unique perspective. Kind of proves he is a true artist, because it happens to all of them."
 — Kay Willingham Shiver, Editor, *Career Pilot Magazine*

Left: *1931 Ford Model A Phaeton*
Right: *1931 Ford Pickup*

"Anthony's Facebook group has bought me so many smiles and inspiration on days I want to just give in, and give up and now thanks to the Schmidt family making this group, instead of looking forward to my two scoops of raisins in my cereal, I am looking forward to my two scoops of Anthony's photography work. Anthony, I truly hope you realize you bring smiles to many different people from many different lifestyles. Keep up the great work and keep knocking down the walls. Never stop doing what you love to do. Thank you, Schmidt family, for letting me tag along on this wonderful journey."

— Micheal Spurling

Top: 1931 Ford Wagon
Top middle: 1931 Ford Model A
Top right: 1932 Chevrolet Roadster
Right: 1931 Chevrolet Truck

1913 Ford Model T

Just Married

Anthony waited patiently more than thirty minutes for the sun to be in the perfect position to get this "Just Married" themed shot of a 1913 Ford Model T driving off into the sunset with the newlyweds.

When the sun finally hit the right spot, Anthony started to snap his pictures and say, "Now we're talkin'."

1940 Ford Pickup

"Our imperfections are the special ways God gave us each a unique way to shine. What a beautiful sunbeam Anthony shares with us."
— Kimberly Davis-Chien

Train Station

The Northwest Railway Museum in Snoqualmie, Washington represents a bygone era, the type of building that once was in every community across the nation. It was the perfect backdrop for this 1949 Mercury Woody and 1950 Studebaker Champion complete with miniature luggage.

1949 Mercury Woody
1950 Studebaker Champion
Northwest Railway Museum
Snoqualmie, Washington

1941 Chevrolet Special Deluxe
Everett High School
Everett, Washington

EVERETT HIGH SCHOOL

Anthony made the front page of the *Everett Herald*, on Tuesday December 7, 2021. The headline read, "He's 13 and famous for photos that make toy cars look real."

There is actually a precise science to forced perspective photography. The distance the model is to the building needs to be exact as does the distance of the camera from the subject. Anthony was a little concerned when a garbage can happened to be in the exact spot he needed to be shooting from, but he improvised and used the top of it to put his platform on.

1937 Studebaker Pickup
Everett High School
Everett, Washington

Above left: 1948 Tucker
Center: 1948 Chevrolet Fleetline
Right: 1949 Mercury Wagon
Everett High School
Everett, Washington

26

1949 Mercury Club Coupe

1940 Ford Pickup
Everett High School
Everett, Washington

Parking Garage

Anthony seems to find the perfect location no matter the weather or time of day. Two convertibles on a rainy day shoot? Most photographers might call it a day and shoot some other time. Anthony makes it work with this genius parking garage photoshoot.

1965 Pontiac GTO
Opposite: 1964 Ford Galaxy

FOOTPRINTS IN THE SAND

On this day at a beach in Kirkland, Washington, Anthony created magic. He had done sandy scenes before and was always frustrated that real sand didn't end up looking to scale. It looked more like larger gravel in this close-up style of photography. That's when he thought of using Kinetic Sand. The texture and the way you can mould it looks very true to life in forced perspective photography. The idea to add the footprints of the driver who had walked away was a spur of the moment addition that takes these photos to the next level.

"Autism, like all variables of the human soul, is just one facet upon the endless kaleidoscope of our character, but autism, unlike so many other of those facets, doesn't just reflect. In the case of autism, that facet is also a window into the spirit, if we could only see past the blinds...there is another infinite universe looking back our way!"

— *Jack McQuade*

Left: 1958 Edsel Bermuda Wagon
Middle: 1953 Buick Roadmaster Estate Wagon
Right: 1949 Ford Wagon
Opposite: 1935 Auburn Speedster

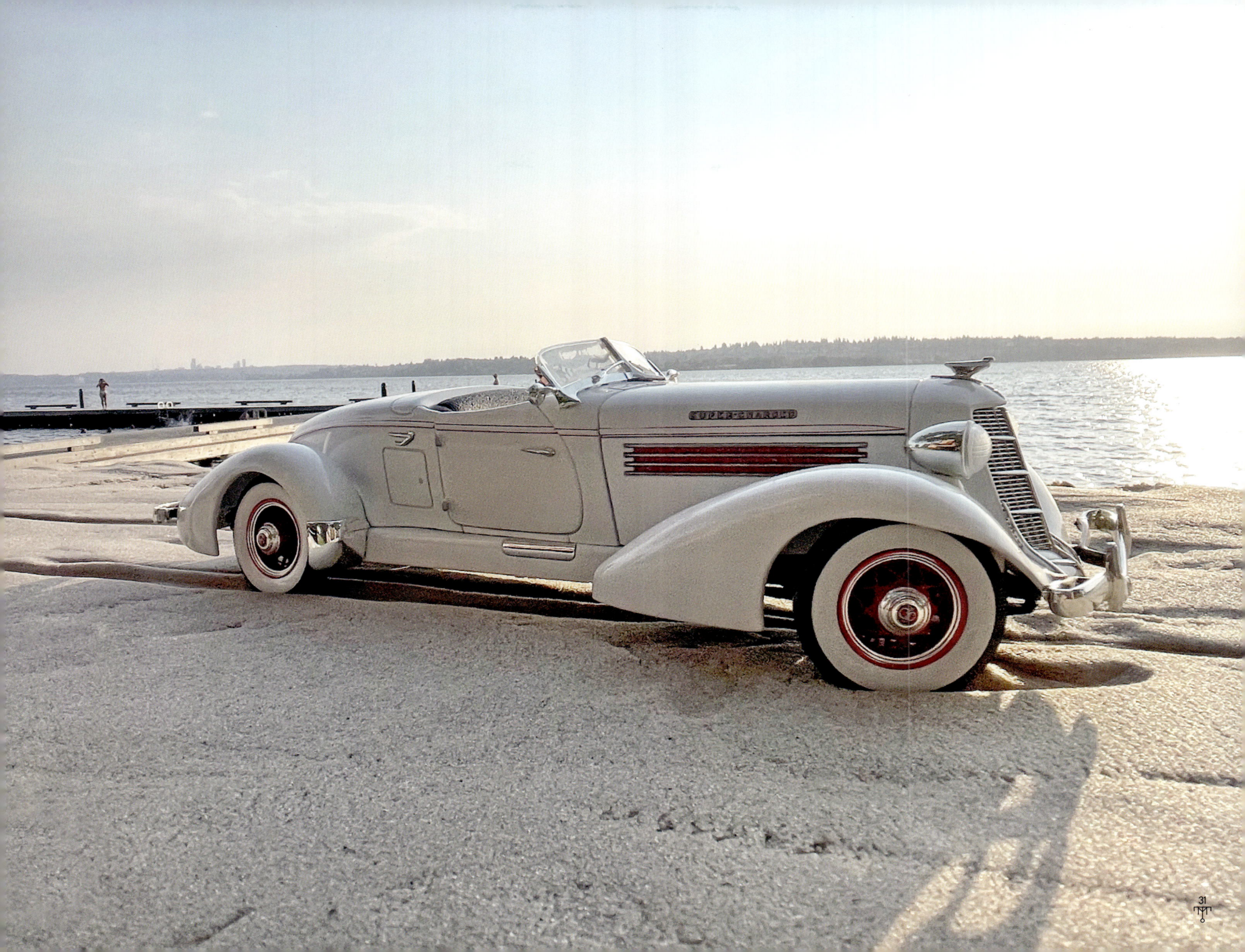

1953 Buick Roadmaster Estate Wagon
1949 Ford Country Squire Wagon

THE BEETLES

Another one of those moments of serendipity, Anthony was shooting this scene and all of a sudden looked up and said, "Do you hear what's playing right now?" In the distance someone was playing the song "Hey Jude" by the Beatles. "What are the odds of that?" he said. "Shooting some Beetles while we listen to the Beatles."

1967 VW Beetle

1951 VW Beetle Convertible

1951 VW Beetle

Firefighter Tribute

September 11th happened long before Anthony was born, but because of his sensitive nature, every year he remembers it. The empty pair of boots you see in the foreground was his way of symbolizing the loss of the firefighters that day.

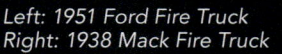

Left: 1951 Ford Fire Truck
Right: 1938 Mack Fire Truck

Left: 1954 Mercedes 300 SLR
Right: 1951 Jaguar XK120C C-Type

DIRT TRACK

In this race car photoshoot, Anthony had his assistant (mom) throw dirt to get the effect of racing on a dirt track. He got pretty dirty, but the results were so worth it.

1965 Ford Thunderbird
Redmond Elementary School
Redmond, Washington

1967 VW Beetle
Redmond Elementary School
Redmond, Washington

1960s Theme Photoshoot

Redmond Elementary School
Redmond, Washington

1957 Chrysler Imperial
Nardoland
Maltby, Washington

NARDOLAND

NBC Nightly News featured Anthony, and what better place to showcase Anthony's talent than Nardoland, home of Ron and Sally-Jo Nardone. Anthony and Ron became good friends when Anthony appeared on *Eric's Heroes* on *KOMO News in Seattle*, and they have an open-door policy for Anthony to come shoot anytime he likes. Anthony was able to get this photo of a model 1957 Chrysler Imperial, in perfect perspective to his life-sized 1959 Studebaker Silverhawk.

WHEEL HUB PHOTOSHOOT

Robert McGaffin from *Wheel Hub Magazine* flew out to Seattle from Madison, Wisconsin just to do a feature on Anthony. He has a personal connection to this story because two of his sons have autism. Robert said, "We get to work with some of the greatest artists in the industry, but sometimes, someone just blows us away. Anthony Schmidt creates life-like dioramas from scale models and tweaks the perspective to make them appear full-size against full-size backdrops. Look for our full feature on this guy and his work. Incredible!"

1948 Ford Woody Wagon
Cottage Lake
Woodinville, Washington

XXX Root Beer

José Enciso, owner of XXX Root Beer in Issaquah, considers Anthony family and his place is Anthony's second garage. They host car shows every weekend. The very first episode of *Eric's Heroes* featured his story growing up in the 1950s when things were not so easy for immigrants. His story is incredible, and he clearly loves the USA and is living the American Dream.

Left: 1956 Buick Riviera
Top center: 1957 Mercury Turnpike
XXX Root Beer
Issaquah, Washington

BURGERMASTER

Anthony had been planning this photoshoot for months. He waited a long time for the weather to improve; it rains a lot in the Pacific Northwest during the spring and everything had to be perfect. He insisted we drive his 1959 Studebaker Silverhawk to the shoot. He loaded the car the night before with four big baskets loaded to the brim with his very best models to fit the era of when the restaurant was built. He had to wake up very early to be there before the restaurant opened so he wouldn't have modern cars in the way to ruin his illusion. He spent three hours taking pictures, and as customers began to arrive, we moved to where the big sign was; that's where he captured this image—the cover of his 2023 calendar.

1959 Dodge Royal Lancer
Burgermaster
Bellevue, Washington

1957 Ford Fairlane
Burgermaster
Bellevue, Washington

Left: 1956 Chevrolet Bel Air
Right: 1957 Chevrolet Utility 150 Coupe
Burgermaster
Bellevue, Washington

"You have an amazing son. He proves that a diagnosis doesn't define or limit who we can become or how big our aspirations can be. Thank you for sharing Anthony with us. Your message and his unique tenacity bring hope and light to a world touched by darkness."

— Dana Lynn Darin

Right: 1957 Buick Roadmaster
Bottom right: 1950 Ford Shoebox Police Car
Burgermaster
Bellevue, Washington

Left: 1961 Pontiac Catalina
Center: 1950 Oldsmobile Super 88
Right: 1959 Dodge Royal Lancer
Regal Crossroads Cinema
Bellevue, Washington

54

A Night at the Movies

Top left: 1950 Oldsmobile Super 88
Top center: 1959 Dodge Royal Lancer
Top right: 1958 Buick Limited
Regal Crossroads Cinema
Bellevue, Washington

WAREHOUSE DIORAMAS

Anthony takes photos every single day without fail, and with our rainy Seattle weather, it's great to have indoor dioramas for when the weather outside isn't the best. The one below was built by Phillip Crews, and the one on the next page was created specially for Anthony by the talented miniaturist Craig Fleck of Wetwork Kustoms. The way the light beams in these miniature buildings is magical, and Anthony puts them to good use daily.

Top left: 1953 Chevrolet Bel Air
Bottom left: 1951 Studebaker Champion
Above: 1969 Ford Mustang GT

1951 Hudson Hornet

1940 Ford Super Deluxe

Left: 1959 Chrysler New Yorker
Center: 1958 Cadillac Fleetwood

1958 Ford Fairlane

1953 Chevrolet 3100 Tow Truck
1940 Ford Super Deluxe

SNOW

It doesn't snow often in Woodinville, Washington, but when it does, Anthony will be out taking photos. He uses baking soda for snow because, believe it or not, real snow has much too large particles and looks out of scale. Baking soda gives a much more realistic snow effect and won't melt if you are working in warmer temperatures.

1986 Audi Quatro

Left: 1923 Duesenberg SSJ
Right: 1937 Studebaker Coupe
The Wickers Building, Heritage Park
Lynnwood, Washington

HERITAGE PARK

The Wickers Building, built in 1919, was the first mercantile and post office on North Trunk Road in Alderwood Manor (now Lynnwood), and became a familiar landmark halfway between Seattle and Everett to passengers on the railway. Anthony's photography is a step back in time against this gorgeous Tudor architecture.

Right: 1913 Ford Model T Panel Van
The Wickers Building, Heritage Park
Lynnwood, Washington

Port Townsend

Anthony saw this beautiful home online and was inspired to do a photoshoot there. So we made the trip to Port Townsend, Washington, which was a long drive including a ferry ride. Thankfully, the homeowners were home so we could ask permission. Homeowner Darren Barrett was so impressed he even tried his hand at taking a few photos himself.

1925 Ford Model Ts
Port Townsend, Washington

Left: 1975 Plymouth Fury Police car
Top: 1976 Chevrolet G20
The Cut Shop
Woodinville, Washington

THE CUT SHOP

A local Woodinville restaurant, the Cut Shop, is '70s-themed. Of course, Anthony decided to shoot era-specific cars out front.

Anthony is a regular at the restaurant. On one visit, we had another of those moments of serendipity. As we sat down at our table, we overheard someone at the next table talking about his photography. Anthony turned to them and said, "Hey, that's me!" Their jaws all dropped and they said, "Oh my gosh, is that you? I can't believe I just met a celebrity!" Everyone laughed and agreed it was the highlight of the day. What were the odds he would sit down right next to them at that exact moment?

ON THE SLOUGH!
425-408-1173

1969 Buick Electra
The Cut Shop
Woodinville, Washington

WOODINVILLE

ON THE SLOUGH!

Left: 1971 Buick Riviera
Right: 1976 Chevrolet G20

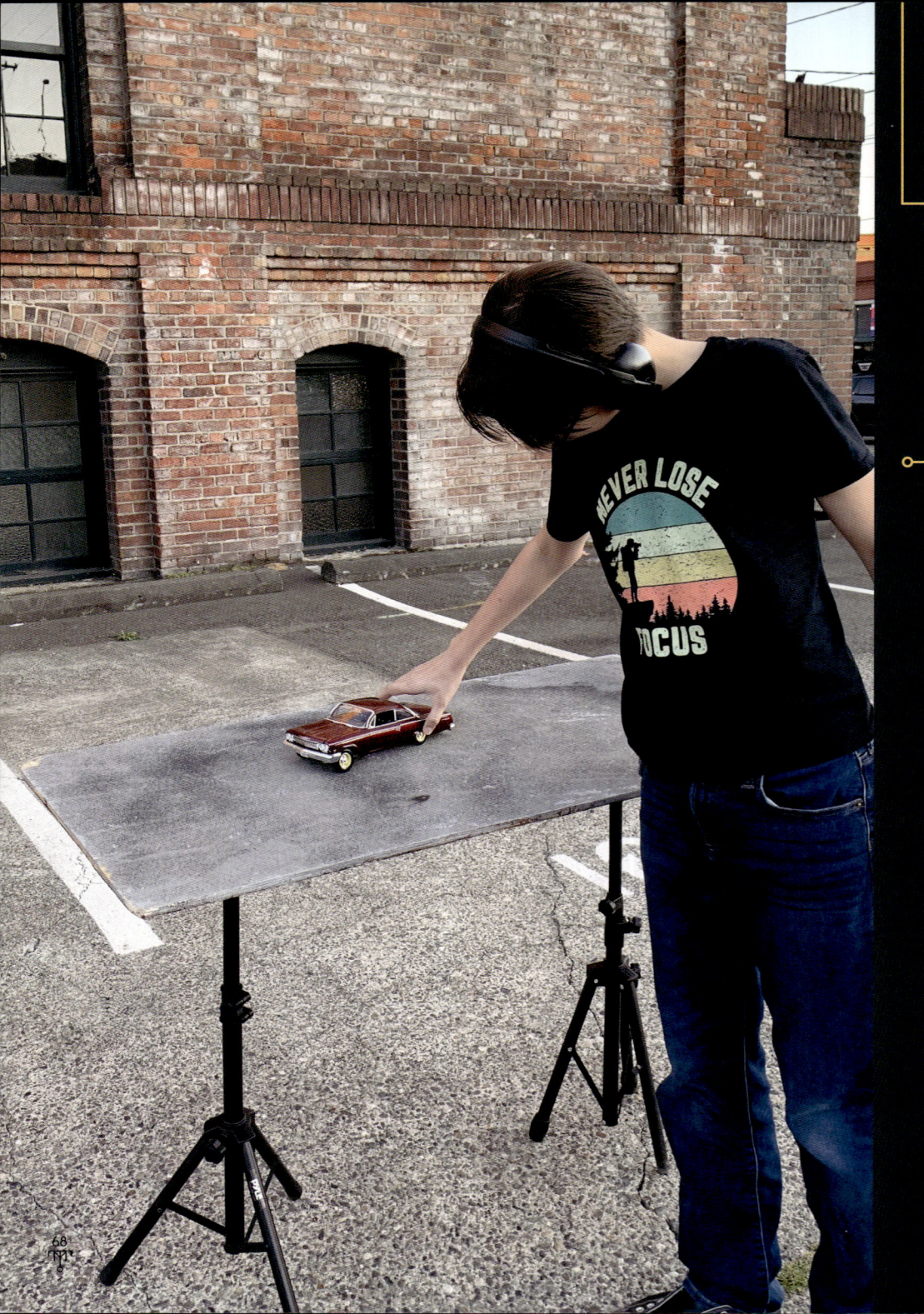

LOW RIDER

This day the theme was Lowriders, so we drove to Seattle, to an area that would be considered the natural habitat of these awesome cars. Anthony was thrilled when not just once but twice we saw real life lowriders drive by. It was one of those moments that seem to always happen to Anthony when everything just seems to fall into place.

"I have been blessed to see Anthony's progress and growth as an artist almost from the very beginning. This has become the proverbial snowball effect in a very positive and stunning way. He has grown exponentially as an artist and young man. Looking at these pictures now, I notice a very profound change. His use of natural light and color is sheer genius in my opinion. They are more than just a picture. They are a moment in time past, present, and future. And for all of us, they stir up memories of days gone by and possible days ahead. Anthony has become the keeper of the keys, as it were. With his vehicles and camera, he can take us anywhere his imagination wants. And he does it with a style that is truly all his own."

— *William Houser*

1962 Chevrolet Bel Air Bubble Top

1969 Buick Electra

THE HOOPTIE

Anthony had the good fortune of running into Sir-Mix-A-Lot at a local car show, Redmond Exotics. Anthony knew exactly who he was and ran up to him to introduce himself. His reaction was, "Hey, my real name is Anthony too!" So, we gave him one of Anthony's calendars and he liked it because he's also a big car enthusiast.

Anthony was then on a mission to do a tribute photoshoot featuring the Hooptie from Sir-Mix-A-Lot's music video for "My Hooptie." The only problem was the model for a 1969 Buick Electra is very hard to find, and the search turned out to be tougher than expected. Anthony let his followers know that he was on the lookout, and that's when Harold Weinstein stepped in and saved the day. He managed to track one down on eBay, and after a bidding war, won the model for Anthony, just in time to surprise him with it for his birthday. Anthony was thrilled, and when it arrived, he went straight to work distressing it and making the tires mismatched just like the real-life version of the Hooptie from the video. I think you will agree he did a great job capturing the essence of that iconic car.

2010 Ford Crown Victoria

1974 Dodge Monaco

Whiteside Towing

Gene Whiteside owns a junkyard and towing company and is Anthony's good friend. Visiting the junkyard is like a trip to Disneyland for Anthony, and Gene always has a special surprise; he even arranged to have Anthony there on car crushing day and allowed Anthony to do the honors of pressing the button on the remote control to crush some cars. It was a day he won't soon forget.

Left: 1949 Ford Custom
Whiteside Towing
Snohomish, Washington

Top right: 1949 Ford Custom
Bottom right: 1956 Chrysler 300

The car community lost one of its best in 2022. Dean Mathews, owner of Dino's Auto Care, was the type of guy everyone loved and looked up to, including Anthony. He'd been taking care of Anthony's car "Betty," the 1957 Ford Custom 300, for eleven years, even before Anthony owned it. One memory of Dean sticks out in my mind, the first time we took Anthony's '57 Ford in for repair. As I reached into my purse to pay, he said, "Put that away; this one is on me." He just loved Anthony, and his garage had an open-door policy for Anthony to come and go as he pleased. He will be greatly missed.

1957 Chevrolet Bel Air
In Memory of Dean "Dino" Mathews

1941 Chevrolet 3100

1957 Chevrolet Cameo
Diorama: Andrew G. Roderick

1969 Chevrolet Camaro Z/28

BIG RED CAMARO

The Big Red Camaro is the fastest '69 Camaro on earth, with its current top speed of 266.2 mph! A father and son project of epic proportions, Dan and RJ Gottlieb started this project back in 1987. RJ has been racing Big Red since he was nineteen and has collected a wide assortment of records and achievements over the past thirty-five years. Anthony was gifted this awesome model car by driver RJ and Team Big Red Camaro. Group 2 Automotive in Woodinville was the perfect backdrop for Anthony's photoshoot.

2016 BMW M6
BMW of Bellevue
Bellevue, Washington

BMW Dealership

The photo that broke the internet. It has millions of views across social media and some people still refuse to believe it's a model car.

2019 BMW M6

RC4WD.COM sent Anthony this remote control Land Rover replica. We drove 2.5 hours to the Columbia River to get the perfect offroad shots.

Big Rigs

Anthony got one of these big rigs as a gift and the other at a local antique shop. He quickly went to work customizing them with an Anthony Schmidt logo on the side. He found the perfect location for his photoshoot at the local Costco. Anthony is getting quite well known in our area, and he was happy to hear several of the shoppers roll down their windows and yell, "Hey, Anthony! We love your work!" as they drove by.

STADIUM HIGH

Anthony's love of art, automobiles, and architecture really show in his photography.

Stadium High School in Tacoma, Washington, originally began construction in 1891 with the intention of building a luxury hotel resembling a French château. The Panic of 1893, however, brought construction to an abrupt halt when the hotel was faced with financial disaster. It was later purchased by the Tacoma School District and rebuilt after a fire to what we see today. Anthony was inspired by the history of the building; he wanted to do a photoshoot that reflected an alternate universe had it stayed a hotel back in the day. He spent three hours on this shoot and took three large bins of cars with him. Little brother Alex, age nine and also a car guy, made a great assistant. It was such a great location, we had to go back for a second day of shooting. Although the vibe reminds you very much of Harry Potter, the school was actually the filming location for many of the scenes of the 1999 movie *10 Things I Hate About You*.

Stadium High School
Tacoma, Washington

1940 Ford Woody Wagon

Left: 1948 Chevrolet Fleetline

1940 Ford Super Deluxe

1931 Ford Model A

"A label may be for giving a name to a disability, but it is not for purposes of defining the individual, or suggesting limitations. I believe Anthony to be an ambassador of autism, and filling a role in his unique community of leadership. He is an excellent example of accomplishment."

— Steve Wicke

Right: 1957 Chevrolet Bel Air
Below left: 1957 Cadillac Eldorado
Below right: 1954 Cadillac Eldorado

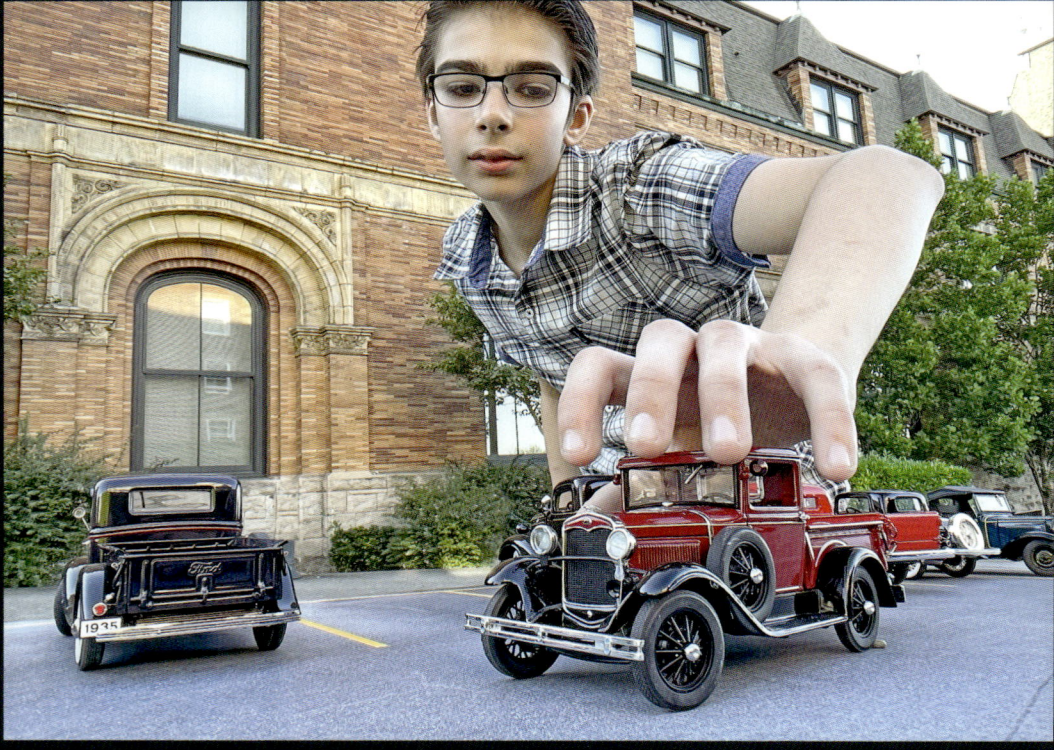

"Anthony's photos touch my soul in many ways. They give me a sense of peace in these chaotic times. They give me strength to keep following my path in life, whatever that may be. When I look at his photography, it puts a smile on my face. Then I imagine him completely engulfed in his imagination and creativity without any reserve. You have shared his world, his talents, your struggles and successes with complete abandon, stepping through fear and hardships with perseverance, faith, hope, and grace. I feel blessed and grateful. "

— Lisa Cordtz

School Parking Lot Series

Anthony came up with the concept of his School Parking Lot series over the summer of 2021. His idea was to do the evolution of the school parking lot, each decade of vehicles with a matching building dated to that same period. It is interesting to see how vehicle styles changed through the years as well as car designs and how they seem to complement each other. The photography turned out to be some of Anthony's best work and very educational too.

The first one in the series was taken at Everett High School, established 1880. The Benz Patent-Motorwagen, built in 1885 by Carl Benz, is widely regarded as the world's first automobile. Anthony likes to tell the story about how Carl's wife Bertha was instrumental in automotive history by demonstrating its feasibility in a trip from Mannheim to Pforzheim in August 1888. Anthony says, "We might not be driving cars today if it hadn't been for a woman who refused to give up."

Anthony enjoys a good underdog story, and let's face it, a story is much more interesting when you share the trials and hardships along the way. It makes the success story that much sweeter; it's another reason we share Anthony's autism story along with his photography.

1885 Benz Patent-Motorwagen

95

1890S ON THE WAY TO SCHOOL

There is no school building in this photo. Anthony imagined heading down a dirt road on the way to a one-room schoolhouse back in the early days of horseless carriages.

1893 Duryea Horseless Carriage

1900S SCHOOL

At the Good Shepherd in Seattle, a historical building built in 1906 was originally a school and residence for young women. I can't imagine they had a 1904 Mercedes and 1907 Rolls Royce Silver Ghost picking them up from school, but we can dream, right? Cars in this decade were mostly only for the wealthy; it wasn't until Henry Ford came along with the Model T that the working man could even dream of owning a car.

Top: 1907 Rolls Royce Silver Ghost
Right: 1905 Mercedes

Above left: 1911 Stanley Steamer
Above right: 1913 Ford Model T
Hollywood Schoolhouse
Woodinville, Washington

1910s School

Hollywood Schoolhouse in Woodinville, Washington was built in 1912. The large brick building operated as a school for only a few years before closing due to a lack of students.

1920s School Parking

Stadium High School in Tacoma, Washington is the perfect backdrop for Anthony's 1920s theme photoshoot complete with Henry Ford and a group of 1925 Model Ts. It almost gives you a sense of what it might have looked like in its early days had it stayed a hotel.

Above you will see a ritzy pair of visitors: a 1928 Mercedes-Benz and 1925 Hispano.

Top left: 1928 Mercedes-Benz
Top right: 1925 Hispano
Stadium High School
Tacoma, Washington

Right: 1925 Ford Model T
Stadium High School
Tacoma, Washington

1932 Cadillac V16

1930s School Parking Lot

The original building of Redmond Elementary was built in 1922, a fitting backdrop for the 1930s vehicles from back when the building was new. Although I imagine some of these wouldn't have been daily drivers back in the day. Perhaps the principal had a side job we don't know about.

1931 Ford Model A
Redmond Elementary School
Redmond, Washington

1936 Ford Super Deluxe

Center: 1932 Chevrolet Roadster

Left: 1948 Tucker Torpedo
Right: 1948 Chevrolet Fleetline
Lincoln Elementary School
Mount Vernon, Washington

1940s School Parking Lot

Lincoln Elementary School in Mount Vernon, Washington was built in 1938. The Art Deco styling really mirrors the car designs of the 1940s. Anthony snapped a 1948 Tucker and 1948 Chevrolet Fleetline in front of the school. Below is a 1949 Mercury Club Coupe and again the 1948 Tucker with some other cars from the era filling the rest of the parking lot. Anthony spends a lot of time setting up the perfect shot, not to mention this location was more than an hour's drive from home.

Bottom left: 1949 Mercury Club Coupe
Bottom right: 1948 Tucker Torpedo
Lincoln Elementary School
Mount Vernon, Washington

1950s School Parking Lot

Eckstein Middle School in Seattle opened as a junior high in 1950. If you have a very keen eye, you will notice a time traveler in this set. Not only is Anthony a talented photographer, but he has a great sense of humor.

Redmond High School
Redmond, Washington

110

1960s School Parking Lot

Redmond High School was built in 1964. Although it was added on to and renovated, they did a great job of keeping that 1960s architectural vibe. These were the first photos to go viral on TikTok.

1961 Ford Country Squire

1977 Dodge Monaco
Leota Middle School
Woodinville, Washington

1970s School Parking Lot

Leota Middle School, built in 1978, is the epitome of 1970s architecture. Anthony does a great job bringing to life the essence of the era, complete with a 1972 AMC Gremlin and 1977 Dodge Monaco.

1973 VW Beetle

1979 Ford F150

Top: 1971 Ford Pinto
Center: 1977 Dodge Monaco
Right: 1972 AMC Gremlin
Leota Middle School
Woodinville, Washington

1983 GMC Vandura

1980s School Parking Lot

The A-Team dropped in at this retro parking lot scene. I pity the fool who doesn't like this series of photos.

Top left: 1989 Mercedes-Benz 500 SL
Top center: 1985 Chevrolet Camaro
Top right: 1983 GMC Vandura
Above: 1980 Mercedes-Benz 500 SL

1990s School Parking Lot

Every car seems to have a story in this set photographed at Timbercrest Middle School, in Woodinville. I wonder if the principal drives the Bentley? The addition of the minivan is a nice touch, something you would definitely see at a parking lot during after school soccer practice.

2000s School Parking Lot

The era we all remember burned in our recent memory. It's hard to believe this era was twenty years ago.

Wellington Elementary located in Woodinville, Washington.

2010 Toyota Rav4
Skyline High School
Sammamish, Washington

2011 Saab 94X
Skyline High School
Sammamish, Washington

2010s School Parking Lot

Skyline High School in Sammamish, Washington was the location for Anthony's most expensive photoshoot yet. Many of these models are extremely rare and hard to get because they are not available in the USA. He even tracked down a replica of our daily driver, a 2010 Toyota Rav4. The 2011 Saab 94X crossover is extremely rare; I'm not sure what's more rare, the model or the real car. There were only 1300 made of the real car and only 600 in the United States.

Left: 2015 Ford Explorer
Center: 2010 KIA Rio
Right: 2006 KIA Carnival
Skyline High School
Sammamish, Washington

Left: 2020 Tesla Model S
Right: 2023 Mercedes-Benz EQS

2022 School Parking Lot

Here we are in our modern era. This looks just like every parking lot you see today, more Teslas than you can shake a stick at. Anthony often laments about the lack of style in modern cars. Even so, the true car guy that he is, he still loves them all.

Left: 2020 Tesla Model 3
Bottom left: 2021 Ford Bronco

1959 Studebaker Silverhawk
Helen Keller Elementary
Kirkland, Washington

INSPIRING THE NEXT GENERATION

Anthony was asked to come speak to Mrs. Seabrook's third grade class at Helen Keller Elementary. After Anthony's speech and car history lesson, the class all lined up for an autographed calendar. Afterwards, Anthony took them outside to have a seat in his 1959 Studebaker Silverhawk.

Mrs. Seabrook said, "As a mother of a son with autism, I sometimes struggle to find words to describe our family's journey and how hard we try to see things through his perspective. I appreciate the ways in which you voice your family's journey and the obstacles that Anthony has encountered along the way. We all need to support and encourage each other, and challenge both ourselves and others to look at the world through others' eyes and perspectives. Only then can we achieve true acceptance and appreciation for others' gifts."

WALT'S LAST RIDE

Eric's Heroes featured a story on Walt Timpe, whose final wish was a ride in a 1976 Cadillac. Anthony saw the story and felt a connection to the fellow car guy and created a photo just for him of his dream car, and paid Walt a visit to give it to him in person. Anthony brought his 1957 Ford to show Walt, and although he was getting weaker and not steady on his feet, Walt made the effort to stand up and peer inside the engine and talk cars with Anthony. We were so glad these two had the chance to meet because only a few weeks later we heard the news that Walt had passed away. Walt's wife Kathy called to let us know that Walt had decided to give Anthony his collection of diecast cars, including some very special ones Walt had built when he was Anthony's age. Anthony treasures them and took photos of every single one. This is one of the photos he took the first day he brought the cars home. What a special way for Walt's memory to live on.

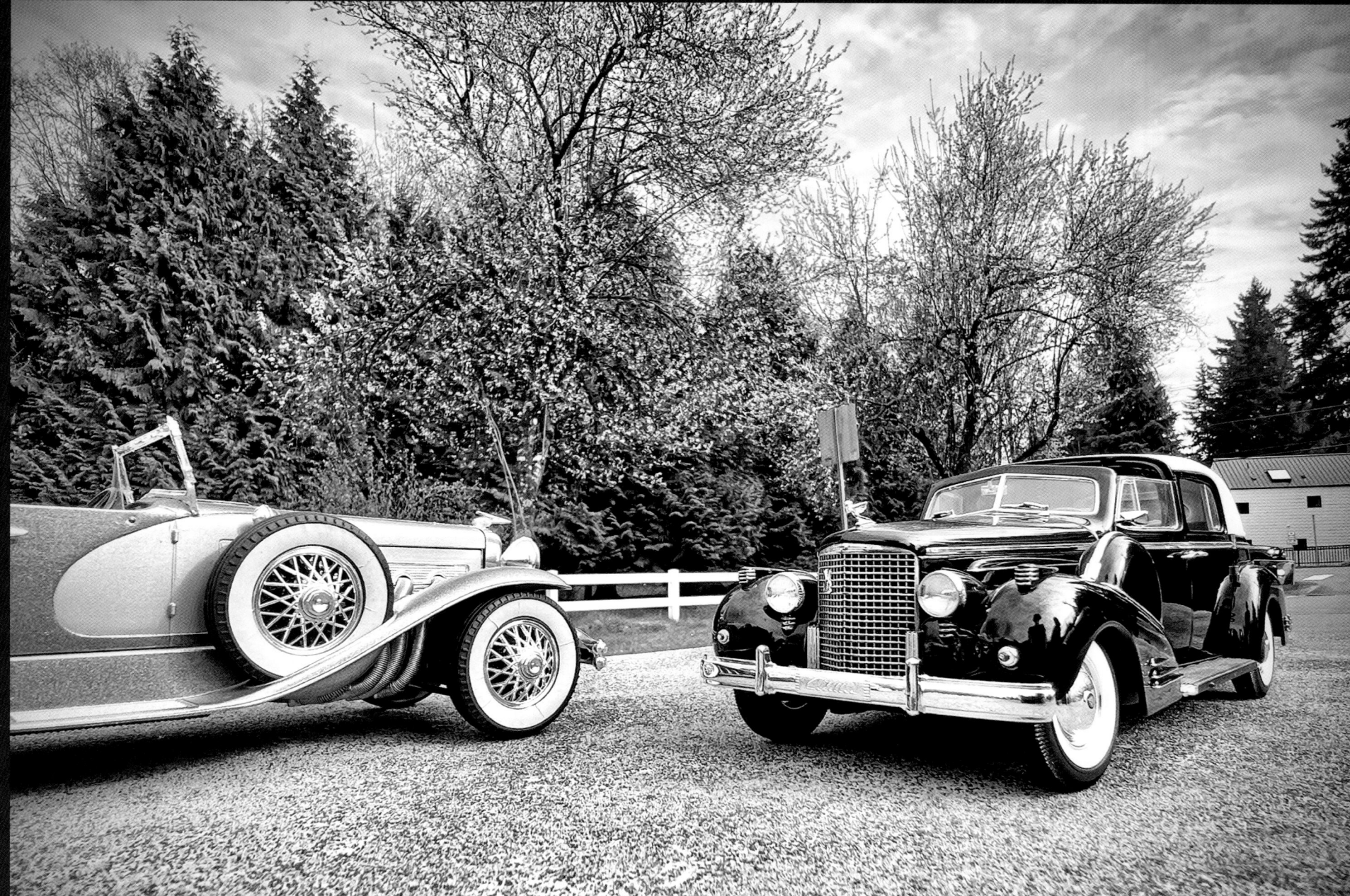

Left: 1932 Duesenberg J
Right: 1938 Cadillac V16

The Journey of the Traveling Pump

A story of epic proportions, that started in April of 2021. Tim Richardson heard about Anthony's man cave plans. So, he went on a hunt to find an antique gas pump. In his search, he asked Stephen Foxall if he had any for sale. Stephen, after hearing Anthony's story, said he had one he would give him for free. The only problem was the pump was all the way in Quincy, Illinois, and that's a long way from Seattle. Tim went to work on how to get it to Seattle. He found out there was trade show in Newport, Tennessee, that all the collectors from all over the country were traveling to, and after a lot of asking around, he found some nice men, Jeff Lemuel and TJ Summers, who were going to that trade show too, and they offered to bring it back with them to Seattle.

Chuck Tamburello of Gorilla Carburetors was so moved by the story of the traveling pump that he offered to do a complete restoration on it.

He gathered his team together, including the best paint and body guy in the area, Curt Moore, to repaint it. No detail was missed and it was brought back to perfect period condition with all original parts. He had a little difficulty tracking down some parts because he didn't want any reproductions going into this restoration. He tracked down Big Mike Auckland, whom Chuck describes as a guy you wouldn't want to meet in a back alley, but with a heart of gold. He found the rare parts and even took some off his personal pump to make it right for Anthony and wouldn't take a penny for his trouble. This was something special that will never be forgotten, and Anthony will treasure that pump forever.

First Solo Art Gallery Show

April is Autism Awareness month. In its honor, Kolva-Sullivan Gallery in Spokane featured Anthony for his very first Solo Art Gallery Showing. Owner Jim Kolva and his wife Pat Sullivan invited Anthony after fellow artist Tom Froese suggested they check out Anthony's photography. A portion of the proceeds from the sale were donated to Ben's Fund, a wonderful charity that benefits people with autism.

People arrived in droves to the opening. Anthony was very professional greeting and speaking with people and signing autographs. Assistant Curator Jennifer LaRue was amazed by the turnout and fanfare. The highlight of the day was the Pharoahs Car Club of Spokane, WA & CDA, ID organizing a cruise past the gallery. It made Anthony's day! It's a testament to how the car community comes together to honor its own.

Anthony's gallery showing even caught the attention of Tim Cook, CEO of Apple, and he tweeted about Anthony on April 2, 2022, World Autism Awareness Day.

Kolva-Sullivan Gallery
115 South Adams Street
Spokane, Washington

From the age of six, Anthony has expressed his love for photography. He now shares his larger-than-life iPhone images of model cars with fans around the world and his creativity really shines through! #ShotOniPhone #AutismAcceptanceMonth 📷 IG: anthony_ryan_schmidt

1:19 PM · Apr 2, 2022 · Twitter for iPad

We were heading out of the gallery to go check out the classic cars that the Pharoahs Club brought by to show Anthony. Peeking in the window of the gallery was a homeless young man, loaded down with a backpack and all his worldly belongings. Anthony stopped dead in his tracks and started up a conversation. The man complimented Anthony on the photography as he peered in the window in amazement.

There's one thing I've noticed about people with autism—they rarely mince words or are shy to ask a socially awkward question. Anthony's curiosity got the better of him and he asked, "Are you homeless?" The man answered, "Yes." Anthony then asked, "How did you end up homeless?" The man smiled at the question that anyone else would likely not have the nerve to ask. "Well, I made a lot of mistakes in my life. Every time I said yes, I should have said no, and every time I said no, I should have said yes." Meanwhile, the entire car club was waiting up ahead for Anthony while he finished his conversation with the man. They said goodbye and the man waved and said, "Good luck with your show."

Homelessness is a subject that Anthony thinks about a lot; he sometimes worries it might happen to him. It was such a sweet moment to see him stop to talk with the man, this fourteen-year-old young man dressed in his suit and tie. Truth is it can happen to any of us, but I think the worry is greater for people on the spectrum because life has given them extra hurdles.

On the night of Anthony's gallery show in Spokane, we were staying at the Davenport Hotel, and after the show Anthony and I were on our way to dinner. As we walked through the foyer, someone noticed Anthony all dressed up, stopped us, and asked, "Special occasion?" I said, "Yes, it's Anthony's first gallery show of his photography." Allan Scott Silbadahl, employee of the Davenport, then said, "I have been looking for you." He handed Anthony a Hot Wheels-sized truck that he had painted with patina himself. "I have a gift for you," he said. "I'm actually on the autism spectrum too, and I love cars. My 1977 Ford LTD is parked outside." So, after we stood there for a moment admiring the small car, we all walked outside to peek at his real car. He went on to show Anthony pictures of all the classic cars he had ever owned, and revealed that he had worked in car detailing. He explained how his autism helped him with his work because of his attention to detail.

Scott grew up in a time when they didn't know much about autism, and he started to relate some of the trials of growing up in that era. He and Anthony quickly bonded over cars, and Anthony was so in love with his car that he wanted to buy it, but what car doesn't Anthony want to buy? It was the perfect end to the perfect day; hard to say when we will ever top that.

When asked if he'd mind if we include this story in the book, Scott said, "I would be absolutely honored to have any mention in your book! Meeting Anthony was amazing. I actually forgot the truck I gave him at home that day, drove a few miles and went back and got it, not knowing if I'd meet you guys or if you were even staying at the hotel. So to see you two in the lobby was a great surprise!

"My sister Joy had mentioned Anthony years ago and I was an immediate fan. Being a car crazy boy on the spectrum my whole life, I saw myself in Anthony and was so thankful autism has many voices today. Anthony's art inspires me to express myself in my art and in my life. I love the idea of a future with Anthony Ryan Schmidt art in it. I'm so grateful for the education, exposure, awareness, and 'face' you put on autism. It helps educate people on neurodiversity."

AUTOS AND AUTISM

People marvel at how Anthony is able to capture such detail in his photos; here's why he's able to do that. The way people with autism process information is different than typical; all information comes in all at once. Where typically we are able to sort out information and without even thinking about it, our brains filter out most of the information and focus in on just one thing at a time, people with autism perceive it all at once.

Here's a snippet from a recent study about autism, featured in *Science Daily.* Professor Nilli Lavie, from the Institute of Cognitive Neuroscience at UCL, hypothesized, "People who have higher perceptual capacity are able to process more information from a scene, but this may also include some irrelevant information which they may find harder to ignore. Our research suggests autism does not involve a distractibility deficit but rather an information processing advantage." So, here's where it gets tricky; while in some instances it can be an incredible advantage, in others not so much. It's the reason why when Anthony was little, he used to melt down in grocery stores. So next time you see a youngster melting down in your local shopping center, realize it's not a lack of discipline.

On the flip side, it can be an incredible advantage. Anthony's friend Austin Riley is a racecar driver with autism and a two-time Radical Canada Cup East Champion. I often see videos posted of him whizzing by other racers on the track, and I can't help but think he has some sort of advantage. When I spoke to him, I asked, "How do you do that?" He told me, "When I'm racing, I feel myself; it's the speed my mind is at normally."

The takeaway is autism is different, not less. These beautiful minds need love, acceptance, and nurturing, and then anything is possible.

Austin Ryley
www.racingwithautism.com
Photo: Richard Hornby
www.releasetheshutter.com

MISOPHONIA

So many people ask, "Why does Anthony wear his ear protection?" They ask, "Is he sensitive to loud sounds?" Not really. He's actually sensitive to everyday sounds that you and I take for granted. It's called misophonia. It is a severe sensitivity to specific soft sounds and visual images. For Anthony, it's chewing and mouth sounds such as lip smacking, also the sound of paper, folding it or crinkling it, or the sound of pencil on paper to name a few.

When a person with misophonia hears the sounds, it causes them to have a very strong emotional reaction such as hate, anger, anxiety, rage, or resentment, and often have an uncontrollable reflex reaction to the sound. The sound directly activates the autonomic nervous system, causing a fight-or-flight response.

Imagine what it's like for him at school, where all work is on paper? Imagine eating in the cafeteria? Gum chewing? Everything that's perfectly normal and common in school becomes excruciating. It's a rare condition even among people with autism. Of all the things he has to cope with, this one is the one I wish I could take away for him. Imagine, every social gathering revolves around sharing food. There's so many missed invitations, restaurants, or even just eating together as a family. It's all not possible. It's important for us to raise awareness about different neurological conditions. It doesn't make someone less than, but at the same time, it's a struggle that people should be aware of, so we can all be a little more kind, a little more understanding of others.

Photo: Morgan Petroski Hjelm

Prosopagnosia

This is Anthony walking away from me on his first day of school. The first day of kindergarten is such a roller coaster of emotions for most of us, but it broke my heart when Anthony recently opened up about his experience.

He shared something I never knew about him. He told me that when he was younger, he experienced face blindness. I had never heard of it, so I looked it up. The medical term is prosopagnosia. I never knew this was an actual thing that some people with autism experience. They see faces in all the detail we do but are unable to recognize faces and commit them to memory.

I used to be very sad during kindergarten. When he was the only kid who didn't come running to their mom with a big hug at pick-up time, I never understood why. He just explained to me what the reason was. He was worried he would run up to the wrong mom! Imagine not being able to recognize your own mother. This made me want to cry because I know he loved me; he was so affectionate at home. How hard that must have been for him. At the same time I'm happy he's developing to where he can recognize us now, because a lot of adults on the spectrum still experience this. He told me that a few years ago when his brother was in Pre-K, he had to look for the boy with the blonde hair and the dragon backpack in the lineup to know which one was his little brother.

What a very smart young man that he's able to articulate his experience and teach us all.

1952 Nash Ambassador
Diorama: Andrew G. Roderick

138
TNT
6

ANTHONY'S PERSPECTIVE

My Workshop

This is where all the cars go to get their repairs done, such as underlighting, suspension work, paint and interior. I often rebuild rusty and old cars and make them look new again. I also patina new ones to make them look old.

In this photo, I am doing a bondo and sanding job on a Chevrolet Impala. I keep my first book *Small Cars, Big Inspiration* on my work bench with my grandfather's old welding mask that was converted to a lamp. He worked at Ford Assembly plant in St. Thomas, Ontario, Canada for thirty years. I have his tag hanging from the lamp, the one he used to use to let the men know he was working in a dangerous spot. He was a repairman at the end of the line. My bench was made from scratch for me as a gift by Bruce Gullian. It has cool V8 symbols, and I think they look great especially with my two classic cars on each side. They both have V8s.

Photos: Morgan Petroski Hjelm

The Collection

I have more than 3500 model cars in my collection, many of which were donated by my followers. I keep them very organized by year and make and model. I also keep a detailed Excel spreadsheet of all of them that I update daily with the current value of each. I always handle them with gloves to avoid fingerprints or damaging the models.

To the right is a picture of my hoarder scene where I display the cars I have painted patina on to look rusty. The little garage was built by Phillip Crews, and Bruce Guillion helped build the tabletop that lifts off. We added the fence and the grass and gravel for this diorama so it's really a team effort.

Photos: Morgan Petroski Hjelm
www.morganpetroskiphotography.com

Photo: Morgan Petroski Hjelm

The License Plate Wall

When my followers heard that I was planning a man cave and wanted to do a whole wall of license plates, they started sending them in from all over the country and even the world! My oldest one is more than 100 years old and is really rusty, and I have a few from Australia and the UK and other foreign countries. Some of them include notes on the backstory that I taped to the back and most have the name of the person who gifted it on the back, too. It makes it that much more special to have in my collection that they came from people who like my photography.

My 1959 Studebaker Silver Hawk

I'm sure most of you have already heard I bought a classic car on Wednesday, January 30, 2022. It might seem a little extravagant for a fourteen-year-old who doesn't even have his license to own two cars, but for me, this will be a lifelong passion of collecting. My first car, Betty, a 1957 Ford Custom, was gifted to me by Greg Wilkinson when I was only twelve years old. I have grand plans to restore her to her former glory. Now that I have made many friends in the car clubs and made going to shows and cruises a regular part of my life, it became clear I would need a second classic to fill the place while "Betty" goes away to be restored.

So, here's the story of how this became a reality. The support from everyone has been amazing. I sold thousands of my photography calendars this year, so we all decided on a budget for me to start looking. The first dealership we went to didn't seem to take me seriously at all. A young fourteen-year-old boy, with sound-canceling headphones, walking into your classic car showroom is likely not a regular occurrence. The salesman was in a hurry to say goodbye and took my information but never sent us a follow-up email.

We waited a week or two before venturing out again to look on this day. We went to a place near my home called Panther Road Classics. The only problem was it was fifteen minutes till closing, and we were about a forty-five-minute drive in rush hour traffic to get there. It might seem reasonable to go another day, but with autism, if something was on the schedule for that day, it's super-devastating to postpone it. I took a chance and called the dealer to see if he was willing to wait for us. I had done all the talking, "Hello, we are on our way to your dealership and wondering if you would wait for us. You have a customer here. I want to buy a car." The salesman was nice enough to say he would wait.

When we got there, the showroom was full of stunning cars; most of them out of my budget. There were a couple in my price range. Then I saw her, a 1959 Studebaker Silver Hawk. What put me over the edge was the price. It was at the low end of my budget, and she was all original and in such perfect shape. It was clear this car had been well cared for. So that was it; I started the negotiations and got the price down to $20,000, and that's a very fair price for a car in this condition. It turns out the salesman knew who I was and was very excited to sell me the car.

I had my mind set on the idea that I would keep it a secret from my dad and brother until we got her home. It was a long several days keeping that secret around the house. It goes to show the character of my father that he trusted us to make the right purchase sight unseen. There was a big reveal in the driveway when we brought her home. I love to do big reveals like that with even the small models I get. So, it all worked out, and my mother helped me settle on the name "Sabrina" after the chauffeur's daughter in the movie with Audrey Hepburn. The name seemed perfect for her, and now she had found her forever home. After we returned home, I said, "Let's get to work. There's a huge dent in my bank account."

Photo: Morgan Petroski Hjelm

1959 Studebaker Silver Hawk
Photo: Morgan Petroski Hjelm

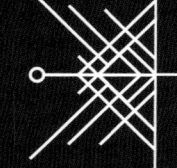

Dioramas Contributed by the Following:

Philip Crews Miniatures

8372 Lawrenceburg Hwy., Mt. Pleasant, TN 38474

931-797-4681

Facebook: Phillip Crews Folk Art Buildings & Miniatures

D. Craig Fleck Wetwork Kustoms

wetworkkustoms@gmail.com

901-218-1543

Instagram: wetwork_kustoms

Facebook: Wetwork Kustoms

Andrew G. Roderick

Andrewredrocket@aol.com

270-303-2216

About the Photographer

Anthony has been changing people's perspectives for a while now. His first book, *Small Cars, Big Inspiration*, had a profound impact on so many people. It can only be imagined what this second book will do. He is inspiring people and bringing them together over the love of cars.

I will never forget one of the most unexpected encounters I had after the first book was published. The dishwasher repairman arrived during our morning scramble getting ready for online school during the COVID-19 lockdown. It was such a hectic and surreal time for everyone. He was admiring "Betty," Anthony's 1957 Ford, parked in the driveway. He obviously was a "Car Guy." After he finished repairing the dishwasher, Anthony gave him one of his books. He opened it up and started reading it from cover to cover! Right there in the middle of my kitchen, this grown man began to cry. He said, "This story is incredible, nothing short of a miracle. I'm a man of faith and I believe stories like this exist to keep us humble. If you think you are capable, or manly, and you hear of what a twelve-year-old with autism can accomplish, it sets you in your place." It's moments like this I savor. As a mom, everything my son does is a miracle, but to see that others feel the same way is indescribable. Anthony's work is just beginning, and he is taking all of us on this journey with him.

About the Cover

Anthony's journey has so many moments of serendipity, and the backstory of the cover photo is a prime example. After the *Eric's Heroes* story aired, I received an email from Jenny C., a friend of one of the producers. She told me that her husband, Dan, was an avid model car collector and that he had recently suddenly passed away. She went on to explain that it would mean so much if Anthony would accept Dan's model car collection. Of course Anthony would treasure them, and the cover photo was the first Anthony took of the cars in Dan's collection on the very day they were gifted to him. It was breathtaking. I knew that moment it would be the cover photo of his next book. I made sure Jenny was the first to see the photo, and she was moved to tears. She couldn't help but think Dan had something to do with that perfect sunset.